PRAYERS AFTER THE HEART OF GOD

BY SKY HIGH PRAISE

Trilogy Christian Publishers
A Wholly Owned Subsidiary of Trinity Broadcasting Network
2442 Michelle Drive
Tustin, CA 92780
Copyright © 2023 by Sky High Praise

Except where otherwise indicated, Scripture quotations are taken from the King James Version of the Bible (KJV). Public domain.
Scripture quotations marked nkjv are taken from the New King James Version®.
Copyright © 1982 by Thomas Nelson. Used by permission. All rights reserved.
Scripture quotations marked niv are taken from the Holy Bible, New International Version®, NIV®.
Copyright © 1973, 1978, 1984, 2011 by Biblica, Inc.TM Used by permission of Zondervan. All rights reserved worldwide. www.zondervan.com.
The "NIV" and "New International Version" are trademarks registered in the United States Patent and Trademark Office by Biblica, Inc.TM

All rights reserved, including the right to reproduce this book or portions thereof in any form whatsoever.
For information, address Trilogy Christian Publishing
Rights Department, 2442 Michelle Drive, Tustin, Ca 92780.
Trilogy Christian Publishing/ TBN and colophon are trademarks of Trinity Broadcasting Network.
For information about special discounts for bulk purchases, please contact Trilogy Christian Publishing.
Manufactured in the United States of America

Trilogy Disclaimer: The views and content expressed in this book are those of the author and may not necessarily reflect the views and doctrine of Trilogy Christian Publishing or the Trinity Broadcasting Network.

10 9 8 7 6 5 4 3 2 1
Library of Congress Cataloging-in-Publication Data is available.
ISBN 979-8-88738-750-5
ISBN 979-8-88738-751-2 (ebook)

Connect with the Author:
https://linktr.ee/SkyHighPraise
EMAIL: skyh68658@gmail.com
YOUTUBE CHANNEL: skyhighpraiseandmeditations

Acknowledgements

My deepest gratitude to the Helper, the Holy Spirit,
whose hovering presence guided, strengthened,
and enlightened me from start to finish.

To my family, whose encouragement genuinely inspired
and supported me every day.

Introduction

PRAYERS AFTER THE HEART OF GOD

This is a book of prayers inspired by the Holy Spirit to draw readers into an intimate conversation and prayer life with God and Jesus, our Lord. *PRAYERS AFTER THE HEART OF GOD* encourages readers to open up and be sincere in the presence of the Lord, as our prayers, requests, and petitions are laid at His feet. *PRAYERS AFTER THE HEART OF GOD* includes a journal guide page so readers can keep a written account of their interactions and responses to deep questions, reflections we may ask of ourselves, and prayer responses from God. These same questions, interactions, and requests can be inquired of ourselves and put before the Lord at different stages and walks of our process of becoming nearer to the God, who loves us. May the journey within this book bring everyone into the deeper relationship of trust, prayer, fellowship, and worship in spirit and truth with the Lord our God.

Prologue

May all who read this book open their hearts to what You desire for them to receive from Your Spirit, O Most High God. Pour out an abundant blessing and endue them with the faith that will lift their power to believe and strengthen their hope to see the unseen. Bring the overflow of Your precious love upon us and draw us near as we surrender and trust in You. Let the prayers of the righteous rise to the throne of your everlasting mercy and grace, and bring forth the manifestation of Your promises to all who call on the name of the Lord. All praise glory and honor be unto You, blessed Father, comforting Spirit, and victorious Savior, Jesus.

In whose name we pray,

Amen

For David testifies to us that, "The eyes of the Lord are upon the righteous, and his ears are open unto their cry" (Psalm 34:15).

May we always remember the times when you have remained steadfast, O God; the times when we looked to Your Word, and it revealed to us that You are from everlasting to everlasting, and You never alter or fade. While our situations and circumstances may change, we give You the glory for being the unchangeable, unmovable, eternal God.

Psalm 90:2 states that "Before the mountains were brought forth, or ever thou hadst formed the Earth and the world, from everlasting to everlasting thou art God."

Reflect: Think about times when God was the anchor in the storm and when He was the one constant source, even when all else seemed unstable.

Pray: Thank You Lord for the promise of always staying, never leaving, and never changing. Help me to stand firm, trust, follow, and obey You in all I do. In Jesus' name.

Share your thoughts on your Reflections:

How did God answer your prayer?

Help us to trust that You have already gone before us Jesus. You have won every battle, fought every war, and obtained all we need to live the abundant life You have planned for us. It is for this reason you came.

Jesus said, "I am come that they might have life and that they might have it more abundantly" (John 10:10).

Reflect: Have there been times when you felt that Jesus carried you through fierce storms and strong trials?

Pray: Help me to remember that You have already traveled this path before me Lord, and every battle has already been won through Your precious blood shed for me. In Jesus' name.

Share your thoughts on your Reflections:

How did God answer your prayer?

We come to rest, dwell, and surrender to the stream of living water springing up for those who desire to partake from the cup of Your saving grace and unconditional love, Lord. Your presence is like healing waters, sanctifying and purifying our hearts. Your arms are wide open and You are available to all who are willing to come unto You and find rest.

God's Word tells us in Psalm 16:11, "Thou wilt show me the path of life: In thy presence is fullness of joy; At thy right hand there are pleasures for evermore."

Reflect: Are there areas in your life where the healing presence of the Lord can bring change and renewal? What are ways you can usher God's presence into your life?

Pray: Lord Jesus, I come to the open arms of Your loving mercy. I submit to You the areas where I am weak or where I have been resisting your intervention and love. Let the waters of lasting change uproot and wash away all the old and renew me for Your glory. In Jesus' name.

Share your thoughts on your Reflections:

How did God answer your prayer?

Give us strength to live in the light of Your promise to us with perseverance and trusting hope, believing that You are able to perform what Your Word assures to us, mighty God. We surrender ourselves to the hands that are strong enough to hold us and to the arms that are open wide enough to carry those in need of endless mercy and saving grace, to the place of rest and everlasting peace.

In Romans 4:21 Paul says, "And being fully persuaded that, what He had promised He was able also to perform."

Reflect: Do you have faith to believe genuinely that God is able to do everything His Word says He can do, as well as all He needs and wants to do in your life?

Pray: Father, Your Word says You cannot lie (Numbers 23:19), so I stand in faith and am convinced, persuaded, and confident that You are the great God who does what He promises. In Jesus' name.

Share your thoughts on your Reflections:

How did God answer your prayer?

Thank You, Jesus, for Your promises made, promises kept, and promises that will be fulfilled according to the divine word of truth. God will answer with a resounding yes as we believe His Word and walk, worship, and rest in Him.

Paul tells the church of Corinth, "For all the promises of God in Jesus are yea and in Him Amen unto the glory of God by us" (2 Corinthians 1:20).

Reflect: When are the times that I have struggled with having faith in God's promises the most? What did I do to build my faith in these times?

Pray: In my submission to the Word, and by faith, let my actions be the amen to the yes that You will manifest because of my obedience in all things. Help me to do Your will, Lord. You are the promise keeper who never fails. In Jesus' name.

Share your thoughts on your Reflections:

How did God answer your prayer?

We are closely held and completely loved in the arms of Your lasting presence, Father. We give You all the glory for the surpassing goodness of Your grace and the tender kindness of Your mercy. You are concerned with everything that impacts our lives and the lives of those who are close and tender to our hearts.

In 2 Corinthians, the Word of God says, "And I will be a Father unto you, and ye shall be my sons and daughters, saith the Lord Almighty."

Reflect: Has there ever been a time when all you wanted was just the Father's love to help you through a situation?

Pray: My heavenly Father, may I feel the touch of Your loving hands around my heart, shielding it, guarding it, and making me stronger. Help me to know You are near. In Jesus' name.

Share your thoughts on your Reflections:

How did God answer your prayer?

Let us always make You our priority, Jesus, seeking You first, setting aside time to abide in prayer and devotion every day. Instill within us a desire to have more of You and to worship and honor You. May we commit to the plan and purpose predetermined for those who are called and cherished by God, and trust that it will come to pass as we believe, bless, and glorify Your name at all times.

David decreed, "I will bless the Lord at all times, His praise shall be continually in my mouth" (Psalm 34:1).

Reflect: Is Jesus your priority? What are some things you can move so that Jesus can come first?

Pray: Life is full of distractions Lord; help me to put You before anything that may cause me to take my eyes off of You. I will remain focused and keep You in the center of my heart, praising you always. In Jesus' name.

Share your thoughts on your Reflections:

How did God answer your prayer?

May the acceptance of Jesus as our Lord and Savior lead to our surrender to Him. Let us yield to the transforming power of the Holy Spirit, deny ourselves, and allow Him to regenerate our mind, will, and emotions to align with the living Word. May the doors to our hearts always be open wide, welcoming and worshiping the worthy Lamb of God.

"If any man will come after me, let him deny himself, and take up his cross daily, and follow me," says Jesus in Luke 9:23.

Reflect: Do you feel the need for more of the Lord, a deeper connection to Him? What are ways you can draw closer to Him?

Pray: Jesus, I surrender all to You and desire a deeper relationship with You. Let there be no closed doors in my life. I expose every area of my life to Your eyes that see through me, see into me, and know every part of my heart. In Jesus' name.

Share your thoughts on your Reflections:

How did God answer your prayer?

The touch of Your caring virtue moves within our hearts and calls us to surrender every circumstance and every burden to You, Lord, for You are strong enough to carry them all and release us to the abundant life where we are free to worship, free to rest in You, and free to love one another as You have loved us.

"Come unto me, all ye that labor and are heavy laden, and I will give you rest," says Jesus in Matthew 11:28.

Reflect: Are there times when you feel like you are carrying the full weight of your burdens? Were you able to give them to the Lord? How?

Pray: Jesus, give me the courage to let go of the burdens that I have been carrying. I want the load to lift, go away, or just get lighter. I know You want me to be free. Help me to come to You in confidence, submitting and surrendering all to You. In Jesus' name.

Share your thoughts on your Reflections:

How did God answer your prayer?

You are the Angel with us; the fire keeping us from the very smell of defeat, whispering words of love and strength to us. You bring us to the other side of every trial, every test, and You continually walk with us as we lean on You and trust in You. May we always keep our eyes focused on the blessed Angel of the Lord who encloses and covers those who fear Him.

David declares that "the angel of the Lord encampeth round about them that fear Him and delivers them" (Psalm 34:7).

Reflect: Do you trust that God is always with you even when you can't feel His presence or hear His voice?

Pray: Mighty Angel of the Lord, I know You fight for me. You surround me like a shield and prevail against all enemies on my behalf. Give me the strength to trust You with my life and help me to keep the eye of my heart focused on You. In Jesus' name.

Share your thoughts on your Reflections:

How did God answer your prayer?

The fire of Your touch Holy Spirit, and Your gentle whisper prompts our hearts to love one another, forgive those who offend us, and to walk in obedience to the Word of the Lord. You are the teacher who guides us into all truth, the refiner who purifies us to be holy, and the transformer who ushers out the old and fills us with more of You.

In John 14:26, Jesus declares, "But the Comforter, which is the Holy Ghost, whom the Father will send in my name, He shall teach you all things, and bring all things to your remembrance, whatsoever I have said unto you."

Reflect: Are there those whom you have felt a prompting to forgive or to show the love of God? Do you need to spend more time in the Word of God, trusting the Holy Spirit to reveal His truth to you?

Pray: Holy Spirit, help me to follow Your leading as You prompt my heart to forgive, or to love, or to give You more of my time in prayer and in the Word of God. In Jesus' name.

Share your thoughts on your Reflections:

How did God answer your prayer?

We overcome because You overcame, Jesus. We are victorious because You are the victor. What a blessing it is to dwell in the glory of His grace and mercy and remain anchored in His everlasting love.

Let our lives be all about loving and serving You, Lord, in spirit and truth, for Jesus said in John 4:24 that "God is a spirit and they that worship Him must worship Him in spirit and in truth."

Reflect: In what areas of your life has the Lord given you victory?

Pray: Thank You for the victory. You are the one, Jesus who gives me the strength now to stand strong and to continue to claim the ground, the territory, and the momentum to continue to walk forward in Your power, serving and worshiping You always. In Jesus' name.

Share your thoughts on your Reflections:

How did God answer your prayer?

Father, let whatever we do in word or deed in Your name be a testimony to the faith that is alive in us with signs and wonders following. May our actions testify and give witness to those we encounter and show that You are indeed alive and the blood of Jesus still has the power to save, deliver, heal, and set free all who are bound.

James states, "Even so faith, if it hath not works is dead being alone" (James 2:17).

Reflect: When was the last time you acted on your faith by stepping out on the Word? What was something that you really took a leap of faith on?

Pray: Help me to have the kind of faith that is alive and pleasing to You, Father, and isn't dead. I declare that I will have the evidence following that will manifest and confirm Your Word. In Jesus' name.

Share your thoughts on your Reflections:

How did God answer your prayer?

You are our Father, and every good thing comes to us from You. You deserve the glory, for You have written our names upon Your heart. We are sealed by the power of Your Spirit through the precious blood of Jesus that was shed for our sins and has reconciled us back to You. Thank You for positioning us to inherit all the goodness that comes to us from being sons and daughters of God Most High.

The apostle John says, "Behold what manner of love the Father hath bestowed upon us that we should be called the sons of God" (1 John 3:1).

Reflect: Am I living as a son or daughter of God, receiving all that God purposed for my life?

Pray: Lord, I want to live as one who truly is in the family of God, ready to be a joint heir with Christ. May I never forget who I am by His sacrifice and live as one who belongs to You. In Jesus' name.

Share your thoughts on your Reflections:

How did God answer your prayer?

We hold on to the hands of Your mercy, love, and grace, mighty God and see signs and wonders of Your power strengthening, uplifting, and carrying us until we believe with all confidence that You are able to bring the pieces of our lives together and create a miracle for those who are Your children. The called, the redeemed, who have received the gift of salvation and now carry the love, the light, and the life of You into the world.

In the book of Romans 8:28, Paul states, "And we know that all things work together for good to them that love God, to them who are the called according to His purpose."

Reflect: Have you had to trust the Lord through a difficult season and believe that it is all working and coming together for your good?

Pray: Help me to remember I am Your beloved child, Lord. Whatever You allow to take place in my life is always operating to benefit me and bring me to a place of maturity and fulfillment in the purpose You have planned for me. In Jesus' name.

Share your thoughts on your Reflections:

How did God answer your prayer?

Let the light You have brought to our lives bring You glory, Jesus, and never be hidden but shine forth as a city on a hill bringing truth, giving strength, and sharing love to all.

Jesus says, "Ye are the light of the world. A city on a hill cannot be hid" (Matthew 5:14).

Reflect: Is my life shining for Jesus? In what ways?

Pray: Show me how to be a light for you, Lord, reveal Your truth and Your wisdom to my heart. I want to let the glow of new life from You be seen by all I encounter each day. In Jesus' name.

Share your thoughts on your Reflections:

How did God answer your prayer?

Our desire is to have ears that hear Your gentle voice speaking to our hearts. Let the continual whisper of Your Word be revealed and received with gladness, as we open ourselves to You,

Sovereign God. Endow us with the wisdom to be sensitive, open, and surrendered, giving You full control of our lives. May we yield and come to know you in the fullness of Your power as you manifest Your love to us through Your caring, comforting presence.

In the book of Mark 4:23, Jesus says, "If any man has ears to hear let him hear."

Reflect: Have I truly given God control of all aspects of my life? Am I listening to hear His voice? Are there areas I hold back from Him?

Pray: I thank You, Father, for giving me the promises of Your Word. I want to give You full control of everything in my life, withholding nothing from You. I place my trust in You. In Jesus' name.

Share your thoughts on your Reflections:

How did God answer your prayer?

Blessed Redeemer, You are the solid ground we can stand on, the chief cornerstone, the rock of ages, a firm foundation, and the anchor for the soul. You are the One who will never let our feet slip. We commit all things into the caring hands of Your generous love, Jesus, for You will work things out for us according to the plan and purpose and promises for our lives.

Paul states, "Being confident of this very thing, that he which hath begun a good work in you will perform it until the day of Jesus Christ" (Philippians 1:6).

Reflect: Do I really trust that all things (good and bad) are working together for my good? What are some things I can do now to help me to trust the Lord while I wait on Him?

Pray: I give you all of my desires, my fears, and weaknesses, Lord. I believe that You love me and that everything is working together for my good, regardless of how it may look right now. In Jesus' name.

Share your thoughts on your Reflections:

How did God answer your prayer?

Holy Spirit, let the outpouring of Your flowing waters rain down upon us and bring life to the dry areas and the parched places of our hearts that need to drink from Your wellspring of life and revive us, refresh us, and restore us.

In Isaiah 44:3 God declares, "For I will pour water upon him that is thirsty, and floods upon the dry ground: I will pour my Spirit upon thy seed, and my blessing upon thy offspring."

Reflect: What areas of my life have become dry and need to be refreshed by the Holy Spirit? Can I truly surrender these things to the Holy Spirit?

Pray: I need to be refreshed, Holy Spirit. Let the fire of Your hands touch my life and bring the fervent desire and true surrender for more of You in my life. Rekindle Your flame within my heart so that I am lukewarm no more. In Jesus' name.

Share your thoughts on your Reflections:

How did God answer your prayer?

We praise You, Jesus, and we await the glorious day when You shall appear and receive to Yourself all those who are redeemed and who trust and believe in Your holy name. We thank You for preparing a place for us in the house of the Father so that where You are, so shall we be forever.

Jesus spoke to believers in Him: "And if I go and prepare a place for you, I will come again, and receive you to myself that where I am, there ye may be also" (John 14:3).

Reflect: When was the last time you meditated and longed for the place that Jesus is preparing for you in heaven?

Pray: Blessed Savior, my heart is filled with joy when I think of what You have done and what You are preparing for those whom You love. Help me to wait on You in expectant hope until I see You face to face. In Jesus' name.

Share your thoughts on your Reflections:

How did God answer your prayer?

All honor and glory belong to You, Jesus. You reign in majesty and excellence, and You give us undeniable love. Look into the depths of our hearts, for we are known by You. Continue to manifest Your renewing power in our lives as we are being changed into Your image and likeness.

In 2 Corinthians 3:18 Paul writes, "But we all with open face beholding as in a glass the glory of the Lord, are changed into the same image from glory to glory even as by the Spirit of the Lord."

Reflect: In what ways am I being transformed into Christ's image? Am I being patient in the process?

Pray: Perfect Your will for my life as I am changing, transforming to be like You, Lord. Give me the grace to trust You as the old is passing away and all things are becoming new. In Jesus' name.

Share your thoughts on your Reflections:

How did God answer your prayer?

May Your thoughts of peace and everlasting good to us give us hope for our future that is planned and designed by You, O God. Let our lives be filled with Your purpose, kept in Your plan, and completed by Your love that leads to eternal life.

Jeremiah prophesied, "For I know the thoughts that I think towards you, saith the Lord, thoughts of peace and not of evil, to give you an expected end" (Jeremiah 29:11–13).

Reflect: Do you believe that God has a special plan for your life? Can you trust Him with that plan?

Pray: My hope is in You, O Lord. I believe the blueprint for my life is held in Your hands. You are the master builder who can be trusted to shape, form, and order every area of my life to fit into Your perfect plan and the divine design You intend for me. Help me to rest in Your peace. In Jesus' name.

Share your thoughts on your Reflections:

How did God answer your prayer?

Guide the footsteps of all who are walking the path to righteousness, and let us take refuge in You, Lord. Surely You will strengthen, shelter, and shield those who draw near to You, for we have been reconciled to You by the precious blood of Jesus. We are sealed and secured by His saving sacrifice.

In Psalm 84:11, David says, "For the Lord is a sun and shield: the Lord will give grace and glory. No good thing will He withhold from them that walk uprightly."

Reflect: Does walking the path to righteousness seem difficult for you at times? Why do you feel this way?

Pray: Even when I don't feel You near, I know You are with me, Father. You have promised to give me Your sufficient grace and a resting place of refuge on the days when I need You the most. I will draw near to You. In Jesus' name.

Share your thoughts on your Reflections:

How did God answer your prayer?

Jesus, You are everything the world is searching for. You are a brother for the lonely, a river of peace for those who seek rest, and healing hands full of virtue for the sick. All glory to You, Holy Spirit, for the power to draw them as the Father calls them, so You, Lord Jesus, will receive them.

Jesus said, "But seek ye first the kingdom of God, and His righteousness, and all these things will be added unto you" (Matthew 6:33).

Reflect: Is the Lord truly what I am seeking? Are my intentions pure and honest toward finding and learning more about God?

Pray: You are all that I need or want, Jesus. Thank You for drawing my heart to You. I want to rest in the assuring waters of Your love, as I seek to know You and flow in the river of Your peace. In Jesus' name.

Share your thoughts on your Reflections:

How did God answer your prayer?

The righteous rejoice, knowing the presence of Your power working in us and for us is only a prayer away. For if we call upon the name of the Lord by faith, we will receive the help that comes from the Father above and is available to us as believers who trust in the Lord.

Paul says, "Now faith is the substance of things hoped for, the evidence of things not seen" (Hebrews 11:1).

Reflect: When you need help do you believe you can call on the Lord to help you? What makes this feel real in your heart?

Pray: I believe in You, Lord. You are my divine help, and I have access to You whenever I need You. Give me the faith to trust that You always hear me and will act on my behalf. In Jesus' name.

Share your thoughts on your Reflections:

How did God answer your prayer?

Your redeeming blood has saved us, Lord Jesus, and has opened the new and living way to eternal life through You. We have been reconciled to the Father; "Therefore, we are buried with Him by baptism into death, that like as Christ was raised up from the dead by the glory of the Father, even so we also should walk in newness of life" (Romans 6:5).

Reflect: Am I walking in the newness of life? How does walking in this way look and feel to me?

Pray: Help me to walk with You, Jesus, while You make all things new, I want to be holy unto You and set apart. Give me strength to let the old things die so the new life in You can begin. In Jesus' name.

Share your thoughts on your Reflections:

How did God answer your prayer?

Heavenly Father, may we receive all of Your truth in love and gentleness of heart, knowing that You seek only to redesign us, renew us, and convert us into vessels of honor that will bring forth the glory of our Lord and King, Jesus. Give us the strength to never fear the refining touch of the fire of the Holy Spirit encouraging us, prompting us, and perfecting us in the way that leads to everlasting life.

Paul writes, "For as many as are led by the Spirit of God, they are the sons of God" (Romans 8:14).

Reflect: Have you had to endure the refining hand of God's power in your life? Do you feel you came through as a better person?

Pray: Father, I know You love me as Your child, and Your desire is for me to be an honorable, treasured vessel. Give me grace to endure Your hand of intervention in my circumstances with patience and hope as You work in my heart and in my life. In Jesus' name.

Share your thoughts on your Reflections:

How did God answer your prayer?

Holy Spirit, Your breath awakens us to a new day, new beginnings, and the "new thing" in our lives, which beckons our hearts. As we arise to Your presence, we are sanctified. Recreate the old man into the new. Transform our minds to be Christlike and reignite us with a flame that consumes and burns fervently, flows endlessly, and empowers mightily.

In Isaiah 43:19 He states, "I will do a new thing, now it shall spring forth, shall ye not know it?"

Reflect: When was the last time you felt on fire for the things of God?

Pray: Spirit of God, bring Your passion into my heart for the things of God, let me feel the fervent desire to be consumed by Your flame that will refine, renew, and regenerate me. In Jesus' name.

Share your thoughts on your Reflections:

How did God answer your prayer?

We honor You, Father, for the garment of praise You provide for us to put on in times of distress or heaviness. It is in Your lovingkindness that You supply them, and also a command for us to clothe ourselves in them. Help us follow and obey, so that weight will be lifted, worry will be dissolved, and walls of doubt, anxiousness, and despair will disappear. May You be exalted over all things whenever we put on our wonderful garment.

In Isaiah 61:3 he says to "appoint unto them that mourn in Zion, to give unto them beauty for ashes, the oil of joy for mourning, the garment of praise for the spirit of heaviness."

Reflect: Do you remember having to put on your beautiful garment of praise? What happened?

Pray: I want to praise You, Lord, in the good times and the bad. When I am weak and when I am strong. You have provided a weapon that will overcome the attacks of the enemy. It is my praise garment. Help me to put it on joyfully, wear it unashamedly, and give You all the glory. In Jesus' name.

Share your thoughts on your Reflections:

How did God answer your prayer?

Lift our hearts to the higher place in You, Lord God. The place where You dwell, and bid us to come rest, and hide when the storms of this life rise against us. Let us have a special fellowship with You in worship and prayer each day, communicating with You as our Father, taking time to hear, listen, and receive what You will speak to us.

The book of Proverbs 4:20 says, "My son give attention to my words, incline your ear to my sayings."

Reflect: How well do I listen to hear what the Lord's instructions or plans are for me in my prayer time?

Pray: Father, I want to hear Your voice and plans for my life. Give me ears to hear and patience to wait on You in every situation. In Jesus' name.

Share your thoughts on your Reflections:

How did God answer your prayer?

Your name is blessed forever, Lord. Sometimes it is hard to express just how deeply we appreciate, acknowledge, and accept the sacrifice of Your life in exchange for ours, the grace You lavish over us, and the love You shower upon us. May our hearts be forever captivated with all of the beauty of Your glory and peace in our lives each day.

In Psalms 29:1–2, David states, "Give unto the Lord, O ye mighty, give unto the Lord glory and strength. Give unto the Lord the glory due unto His name, worship the Lord in the beauty of holiness."

Reflect: How many times daily do you stop and thank the Lord for His goodness and worship Him just because He is God?

Pray: Almighty God, You are awesome. You have loved me with a love so special, so sincere, that I am overflowing with the goodness You bring into my life. Help me to always express my sincere praise and love to You. In Jesus' name.

Share your thoughts on your Reflections:

How did God answer your prayer?

Though we may weep through the dark seasons of life, we shall have an awakening to joy unspeakable and rejoice in the Lord our God as the day dawns. His new mercies will pour over us, like the refreshing rain after the storm renewing our minds, washing and purifying our hearts, and quenching our thirsty souls.

"Weeping may endure for a night, but joy cometh in the morning" (Psalm 30:5).

Reflect: When was the last time you threw yourself a praise session? Worshiping God for His goodness alone?

Pray: I know I have an escape from despair, discouragement, and doubt. It is called praise. As I enter into Your presence, may my praise be the instrument that will bring victory as I lift my heart and hands to You. In Jesus' name.

Share your thoughts on your Reflections:

How did God answer your prayer?

Let us meditate on Your Word, Lord, with our minds focused on the heavenly place, on the things above that are lovely, pure, true, and of good report. The place where angels surround You in adoring worship night and day. May we rest in Your promises while we wait for them to manifest.

"Set your affections on things above not on things on the Earth" (Colossians 3:2).

Reflect: Do you take time to consider the Lord and all of His marvelous works in the heavens, on Earth, and in your life?

Pray: I will purpose in my heart to keep my mind on the things above as You work out the things that I have released into Your hands, Lord. Help me not to worry but to put my faith in You. In Jesus' name.

Share your thoughts on your Reflections:

How did God answer your prayer?

We have access to the perfect place of peace, the precious presence of You, Lord, where we leave the cares of this world behind. It is a place where we can find rest, solace, strength, and the privilege to fellowship and praise the Lord—to gain victory in the freedom that has already been won by the precious blood of Jesus. Let us approach You with boldness as we enter into Your presence to obtain all we need and desire.

Paul exclaims in Hebrews 4:16, "Let us therefore come boldly unto the throne of grace, that we may obtain mercy and find grace to help in the time of need."

Reflect: Is there a special time you set aside to be in the presence of the Lord daily? Are there things you need to rearrange so He can be your priority?

Pray: I need time with You, Lord, to thank You, talk with You, to be still and hear Your voice, and to be reminded that You are always with me. Help me to earnestly make room for this special time with You every day. In Jesus' name.

Share your thoughts on your Reflections:

How did God answer your prayer?

Jesus, You are the vine of everlasting life. May we draw from the never-ending stream that sustains and causes us to live worthy of You, bearing fruit in every good work. And to stay joined, connected, and engrafted to You as our source. You are the gentle Shepherd who guides, nurtures, and shapes us into the new creation that You have ordained for us.

In John 15:5 (NIV) Jesus declares, "I am the vine, you are the branches: If you remain in me and I in you, you will bear much fruit; apart from me you can do nothing."

Reflect: Think of ways you can stay connected to the Lord, the vine who imparts His life, light, and love into our lives.

Pray: You are my connection to everything that is good in my life, Jesus. Teach me how to stay close to You, in communion with You, and consecrated to You each day. In Jesus' name.

Share your thoughts on your Reflections:

How did God answer your prayer?

May our hearts be filled with gratitude and devotion for the sacrifice You made for us, Jesus. The free offer of Your life to pay the price for our lives is incomparable. In return for the gift of Your life to us, let our lives be a dedication of obedience and sincere praise in exchange for Your glorious, eternal act of love.

In the book of Romans 6:23, Paul says, "For the wages of sin is death, but the gift of God is eternal life through Jesus Christ our Lord."

Reflect: What has been your offering to God to show your gratitude for the gift of Jesus Christ?

Pray: I offer You my life, Father, in exchange for the perfect gift of salvation by Jesus because of Your love. May I always overflow with thanksgiving and submit to Your life-saving, life-changing free gift. In Jesus' name.

Share your thoughts on your Reflections:

How did God answer your prayer?

The handprint of Your defining touch is seen in all creation, Father. You count the stars and call them by name. How much more loving are Your thoughts to Your sons and daughters? You have known us from our mother's womb and numbered the hairs on our heads. In Your inconceivable love for us, You gave us the perfect gift of Jesus so that we would have eternal life with You. In return for Your great love for us, let us draw nearer and deeper to You in devotion and dedication with all that is within us.

"You shall love the Lord thy God with all your heart, with all your soul, and with all your mind" Jesus says in Matthew 22:37–40 (NKJV).

Reflect: Are there times when you stop and think of the loving grace that God extends to us as sons and daughters?

Pray: I commit myself to You, Father. I want to love You fully and completely as a sign of my appreciation and gratitude for all You are to me. I surrender all of my life to You, holding nothing back, for You held nothing back from me. In Jesus' name.

Share your thoughts on your Reflections:

How did God answer your prayer?

See into the depths of our hearts, omniscient God. Let the intents and motives be open before You, for you know the ways of man. May the innermost thoughts of our hearts be exposed to the truth of the Word, measured by the love of the Father, and conformed to the life of Jesus our Savior.

"Search me O God and know my heart, try me and know my thoughts, and see if there be any wicked way in me, and lead me in the way everlasting" (Psalm 139:23).

Reflect: When was the last time you were quiet before the Lord, examining your heart, motives, and intentions?

Pray: You are the all-knowing Father, who sees into the deepest parts of my heart and mind. There is nothing kept secret or hidden from You. Lead me in the way of Your truth and righteousness. In Jesus' name.

Share your thoughts on your Reflections:

How did God answer your prayer?

We lift up praise and thanksgiving to you, Sovereign God, for being the answer to every problem, the solution to every situation, and the supplier of all we need. You are the way to life itself and all the goodness it holds. May we become yielded vessels and find strength in knowing, loving, and serving as You prepare us for the divine purpose You will fulfill in our lives, in Your time.

David declares, "But the plans of the Lord stand forever, the purposes of His heart through all generations" (Psalm 33:11 NIV).

Reflect: Has the plan and purpose of God been revealed to your heart?

Pray: Thank You, Lord, for having me on Your mind and preparing a special plan for my life. May I keep my heart open and my mind focused on You so that the path that You have designed for me to walk in will be made known to me in due time. In Jesus' name.

Share your thoughts on your Reflections:

How did God answer your prayer?

Let all that is within us be sanctified by Your Word of truth. Purify anything that is not like You, Lord. May it be burned away in the refining fire of Your Spirit. Keep our feet steady and grounded on the road that leads to everlasting life and Your exceeding love, which is ours eternally. Continue to mold us into vessels of gold and honor for Your divine purpose. In Jesus' name.

Timothy tells us, "Therefore if anyone cleanses himself from these things, he will be a vessel for honor, sanctified, useful to the Master, prepared for every good work" (2 Timothy 2:21).

Reflect: Is the Father reshaping and recreating your life with the refining touch of the Holy Spirit?

Pray: Do what is necessary, Father, to mold me into what You desire. I place my life in Your hands. In Jesus' name.

Share your thoughts on your Reflections:

How did God answer your prayer?

There is no love greater than Your love, Jesus. May we show Your love through a life of obedience to Your Word, and by our genuine praise and adoration for You. Let us be doers of the Word and demonstrate how much we love and honor the sacrifice You made when You died to forgive our sins. May we transfer this same ceaseless love that believes, hopes, and endures all things to others.

Jesus said, "Greater love has no one than this, than to lay down one's life for his friends" (John 15:13, NKJV).

Reflect: Are you showing selfless, unconditional love for others? Can you recall an instance when this kind of love was needed for someone who may not have deserved it?

Pray: All I can say is thank You, Lord. Having this kind of love for others isn't always easy. Help me to remember that You loved me when I was undeserving, unlovable, and unconnected to You. Yet still, Your love was greater for me. Help me to have the same kind of love for others. In Jesus' name.

Share your thoughts on your Reflections:

How did God answer your prayer?

Holy Spirit, You are the refuge for us when the storms of life rise and we find ourselves in valleys of trouble, unrest, or despair. Your covering is the blanket of warmth and security we can rest in to shield us as we go through tests, adversity, or seasons of doubt. Help us to seek the arms of the divine helper sent from the Father to teach, reveal, and guide us in our path as we find strength in Your peace.

"But when He, the Spirit of truth, comes, He will guide you into all truth," says Jesus (John 16:13).

Reflect: Do you seek the help of the Holy Spirit to comfort and guide you in times of trials?

Pray: Forgive me Lord, when I try to handle things on my own, forgetting that all of our help comes from the One sent from You, who is here to walk with me and to see me through anything I may encounter. May I remember to reach for the hands of the help that comes from above. In Jesus' name.

Share your thoughts on your Reflections:

How did God answer your prayer?

Open our ears to the word of the gospel of Almighty God. Prepare our hearts to receive all You have revealed. Let the eyes of our faith be enlightened to see the oppressed set free, the sick healed, and dry bones brought back to life. May our hope and expectation be stirred. Though we have not seen You, we believe in You and trust the Word You have given.

Peter says, "But the word of the Lord endures forever. And this is the word which by the gospel is preached unto you" (1 Peter 1:25).

Reflect: Have you recently had to trust in God's Word when everything seemed to look hopeless?

Pray: Though things may look contrary to the word of life, help me to have patience and wait for You to bring everything to pass, Lord. In Jesus' name.

Share your thoughts on your Reflections:

How did God answer your prayer?

Prince of Peace, we give You all the glory for the beauty of Your lasting comfort indwelling our hearts, calming our minds, and bringing us to the place of stillness—a place we can hear Your voice leading us to enter into Your presence with rejoicing and gladness. Where the manifestation of Your divine love dissolves all worry and dispels all anxiety. You are the solution to the peace many long for; let it flow over us like a river of tranquil waters. May we keep our minds on You as we abide and worship You.

Paul states, "And the peace of God, which passes all understanding shall keep your hearts and minds through Christ Jesus" (Philippians 4:6).

Reflect: Have you sought shelter in the peace of the Lord over an alternative to peace?

Pray: In this world, there are many ways to try to seek peace and tranquility, but Your Word tells us Your peace is perfect and passes all understanding (Philippians 4:6). This is the peace I long for and need. Help me to find it in You. In Jesus' name.

Share your thoughts on your Reflections:

How did God answer your prayer?

Majestic God, we may never come to realize the full measure of the depth of your love, which is inexplainable, the height of Your compassion, which is unreachable, and the width and breadth of Your tender mercies, which are inconceivable, until we see You face to face. We know You sent Your only begotten Son, Jesus, so that whosoever would believe in Him would not perish, but have everlasting life (John 3:16).

Reflect: Have you ever wondered about the love of God for you?

Pray: Father, I am amazed at the generosity of Your love. I desire to have the same kind of compassionate love for others, even when they don't deserve it. May my love to others reveal the depths of Your love for all of mankind. In Jesus' name.

Share your thoughts on your Reflections:

How did God answer your prayer?

Thank You, Lord, for the beautiful clothing that You provide to cover us for the seasons of our lives. You give the robe of righteousness to those who are saints of God. When we display a life of obedience, holiness, and faithfulness for the whole world to see, they will know we are children of God. The garment of salvation is for those who have been redeemed by the Lord. Give us the courage to wear it boldly, faithfully, and unapologetically. May these garments be a continual reminder that You are always with us, and we are eternally Yours through the blood of Jesus. His sacrifice makes us forever free and fully loved.

"I will greatly rejoice in the Lord, my soul shall be joyful in my God; for He hath clothed me with garments of salvation, He has covered me with the robe of righteousness as a bridegroom decks himself with ornaments, and as a bride adorns herself with jewels (Isaiah 61:10).

Reflect: Do you feel like royalty as a member of the household of God and in fellowship with the saints?

Pray: Heavenly Father, sometimes I forget You have called and chosen me. Let me always remember that I am a child of God, who is ever present, all knowing, and whose love for me is undeniable and unmatched throughout the entire universe. May I always remember that I am treasured and highly favored by You. In Jesus' name.

Share your thoughts on your Reflections:

How did God answer your prayer?

Give us strength, faith, hope, and patience to wait for the answers to our prayers, Father. Believing, undoubting, and in faith. Let us not look at the circumstances that surround us, but spend time praising and giving thanks in anticipation that what we pray for we shall have.

Jesus spoke, "If ye shall ask anything in my name, I will do it" (John 14:14).

Reflect: Are you able to praise the Lord and trust Him while you are in the waiting season of prayer?

Pray: Father thank You for loving me, let my faith rise to a new level of believing, as I wait with a heart of praise, trusting You to act on my request and manifest the solutions I need according to Your will. In Jesus' name.

Share your thoughts on your Reflections:

How did God answer your prayer?

In the same way You gave Your life for our sake Jesus, let us lose our lives for You, Lord. When the trials of this life seem hard to bear, we must believe You are near. Though we cannot see You, may we still have the yes in our hearts to serve and follow You.

"For he who seeks to save his life shall lose it, and he who seeks to lose his life for my sake shall find it," says Jesus (Matthew 10:39).

Reflect: Have there been times when you had to say yes to the things of God when you felt like saying no?

Pray: I want to be dead to things of this world and be alive unto You. Develop within me the desire to go after things that pertain to You and to Your glory, Lord. Give me the strength to open the door to more of You and close the doors that lead me away from Your Word and the benefits of the new life promised to me. In Jesus' name.

Share your thoughts on your Reflections:

How did God answer your prayer?

May we surrender all of our battles to the Lord, strong, and mighty, the Lord of Hosts, who will stand for us when we are mistreated or misunderstood, with His gentle hand stretched out to cover us and shelter us while He wins the battle and makes recompense for all wrongs to us. He will always prevail and He has never lost a battle. We are grateful that the undefeated conqueror will always fight for us.

"And all this assembly shall know that the Lord saves not with the sword and spear, for the battle is the Lord's, and He will give you into our hands" (1 Samuel 17:47).

Reflect: Are there some battles you had to surrender to the hand of the Lord? What happened?

Pray: Help me to give all of my battles over to You, Lord God, and not try to fight on my own. I leave them all in Your hands and wait with patience for the victory as You conquer them all in Your way and in Your time. In Jesus' name.

Share your thoughts on your Reflections:

How did God answer your prayer?

Father, You are the one who gives good things to us, who are Your children. Your love, power, and grace surround us and gives us strength and endurance. Your mercies to us are new, and You answer our prayers with new miracles each day. May we be aware of all the new things You do in our lives because of Your love. Let us take advantage of each new moment, each new milestone, every day, and give You praise for all the blessed things You give us.

James declares that "every good and perfect gift is from above, coming down from the Father of the heavenly lights, who does not change like shifting shadows" (James 1:17, NIV).

Reflect: Have you noticed anything new God has been doing in your life?

Pray: Increase my awareness of Your Sovereign hand Father. Help me to see all the new things You are doing in my life each day. Open my ears to Your Word, so I can hear the whisper of Your voice delighting my soul as You tell of the abundant blessings planned for me in the kingdom of heaven. In Jesus' name.

Share your thoughts on your Reflections:

How did God answer your prayer?

You are the bread from heaven, Jesus. You know all we need and how much we can bear. In Your lovingkindness, You will never put more on us than we can carry. We obtain all we need from You as our faithful supplier who is never late and always present to fill us with the divine Word that builds us up and renews our minds.

"I am the living bread which came down from heaven, if any man eats of this bread, he shall live forever" (John 6:51).

Reflect: Are you getting your portion of living bread each day?

Pray: I want to be open to all that You have for me, Lord. Help me to receive my portion of divine nourishment from You each day as I come to You with my hands and heart open. In Jesus' name.

Share your thoughts on your Reflections:

How did God answer your prayer?

Heavenly Father, You spoke the world into existence by the power of Your words. By Your Spirit, You continually water the seeds You plant in our hearts through Your precious word. May the Word take root within us and grow into a tree of everlasting life, bearing fruit that remains. Let there be new life that generates from us, let there be light that shines forth from new creation as we desire more of You and seek You with our whole heart.

"You did not choose me, but I chose you and appointed you so that you might go and bear fruit—fruit that will last—and so whatever you ask in my name, the Father will give you" (John 15:16, NIV).

Reflect: In what ways can you water the seeds of growth and renewal God plants in your daily life?

Pray: I desire to grow closer, stronger, and nearer to you, Father. I know Your Word is the nourishment I need every day to go farther, reach higher, and walk courageously with You. Help me to allow Your Spirit to teach and reveal more of You to me as I surrender and embrace more of You. In Jesus' name.

Share your thoughts on your Reflections:

How did God answer your prayer?

You came down Lord, and took on human form so You could feel, know, and be touched with our trials and sufferings without sin. We know You are the mediator who sits on the right hand of God. Loving, feeling, and in touch with the infirmities of those who recognize You as the high priest who has now passed into the heavens, making intercession on our behalf.

"It is Christ who died, and furthermore is also risen, who is even at the right hand of God who also makes intercession for us" (Hebrews 7:24–25).

Reflect: Do you feel you can bring all of your needs to Jesus, no matter what they are?

Pray: You are the high priest, Lord Jesus, that I come to when I am worried, tired, or in need of divine help. May I come to you without fear or hesitation, with humble heart, and lay all things at Your feet—the place of Your tender mercies and abounding compassion. In Jesus' name.

Share your thoughts on your Reflections:

How did God answer your prayer?

Blessed Redeemer, You laid aside Your divinity and took on human flesh to save us. Your humbleness showed the heart of a Savior, while Your power revealed Your purpose to become the sacrifice for all mankind. Let all those who are lost, all who need Your life-saving gift recognize there is no sin too great and no burden too heavy for the Savior who sought not to save his own life, but rather gave His life, fulfilling His promise then, now, and for eternity.

"For He made Him who knew no sin to be sin for us, that we might become the righteousness of God in Him" (2 Corinthians 5:21).

Reflect: Have you recognized the need for the Savior in everyday life?

Pray: Jesus, You are wonderful. I give thanks each day for Your precious gift of life to me. I know I need you to walk alongside me in this life, letting me know that it is well because I chose to journey on the narrow road with you. Through each day, good or bad, I will stand on Your promise to always be with me. In Jesus' name.

Share your thoughts on your Reflections:

How did God answer your prayer?

Our hope in You will never make us feel ashamed, Lord. For You are true to Your Word, which is the banner of Your faithfulness and fulfills Your purpose in our lives. Give us the strength to endure through doubt, impatience, or worry in regards to the future which You constructed and planned for each of us while we were yet in our mother's womb.

The Lord says, "Before I formed you in the womb, I knew you and before you were born, I set you apart and appointed you as a prophet to the nations" (Jeremiah 1:5).

Reflect: What actions do you take to keep your hope in God's promises alive in your heart?

Pray: Help me to remain hopeful in the plan and purpose that You have for my life, Father. Reveal it to me according to Your Word. Give me strength to endure and patience to trust as You unfold all You have for me, day by day. In Jesus' name.

Share your thoughts on your Reflections:

How did God answer your prayer?

Jesus, You are the bridge to our peace. May we always abide and remain on the road that leads us into the place of experiencing the promises You have made to us, the abundant life of Your goodness, and a deeper intimacy with You. Even if Your path leads us into uncharted, unknown, and unfamiliar waters, we can rest in assurance knowing You will be there with us. You will steady our hearts and fortify our minds as we put our hope in You.

Paul writes, "For He Himself hath said, I will never leave you nor forsake you" (Hebrews 13:5).

Reflect: How do you remain on the road to peace?

Pray: Sometimes the road to peace can be hard to stay on with all the distractions and busyness of life, Lord. Teach me to relax and to give all my concerns to You each day. You will keep me steadfast, secure, and walking in the direction that brings me nearer to You. In Jesus' name.

Share your thoughts on your Reflections:

How did God answer your prayer?

Reigning King Jesus, You are worthy to be glorified in every area of our lives. You see every flaw, every weakness, and every empty area within us, and yet You accept us. Your love is truly unconditional, sufficient, and everlasting. May we continue to walk close to You so we experience the full measure of all You have for us.

In his letter to the church, Paul writes, "To the praise of the glory of his grace, wherein He has made us accepted in the beloved. In whom we have redemption through His blood, the forgiveness of sins, according to the riches of his grace" (Ephesians 1:6–7).

Reflect: Do you recognize the areas in your life that God's unconditional grace and love have overlooked and covered so that He could reveal His love and purpose, regardless of your shortcomings?

Pray: Thank You, Jesus, for seeing me through the eyes of grace and loving kindness. Your plan and purpose extend beyond any frailties or character flaws that I have. May I always remember what You are accomplishing in my life as You move me forward and walk with me into the destiny chosen for me. In Jesus' name.

Share your thoughts on your Reflections:

How did God answer your prayer?

Let us step out into the holy rain of Almighty God. It is falling in abundance. Let it fall into hearts that are open and to those who are thirsty for the living water coming from You. May we be liberated and filled with more of you, Holy Spirit. You know where we need revelation, Your teaching, and Your love. Revive us from the continual fountain of life, and replenish the weak, tired, and weary areas of our lives. Bring lasting hope, unspeakable joy, and complete regeneration.

The Lord speaks, in Isaiah 45:8, "Drop down ye heavens, from above and let the skies pour down righteousness, let the earth open, and let them bring forth salvation, and let righteousness spring up together, I the Lord have created it."

Reflect: Are you stepping into what God has for you?

Pray: Give me the faith to step into the blessings that You have prepared for us, Father. May they fall as the morning dew upon me and remain within me by Your Spirit. Thank You for the way, the truth, and the life, Jesus our Lord. By Him and through Him, we have life eternal, hope unending, and love everlasting. In His name I pray, Amen.

Share your thoughts on your Reflections:

How did God answer your prayer?

179

Epilogue

PRAYERS AFTER THE HEART OF GOD was formed from intercessory prayers for the body of Christ as we go through the process of becoming more like Jesus, our King, and for those who have yet to come to know the saving grace and love of Jesus, our Redeemer. May the compassionate and faithful heart of God be open to all who humble themselves, seek His face, and live righteously before Him as we come to know ourselves and our God. May He grant the petitions declared by faith and trust as we come before Him surrendering all.

In Jesus' name.

Amen.

Printed in the USA
CPSIA information can be obtained
at www.ICGtesting.com
LVHW011431260923
759277LV00008B/158